Crusader Castles: The History of the Medieval Castles Built in the Holy Lands during the Crusades

By Charles River Editors

Shayn O's picture of the remains of Margat in modern Syria

About Charles River Editors

Charles River Editors is a boutique digital publishing company, specializing in bringing history back to life with educational and engaging books on a wide range of topics. Keep up to date with our new and free offerings with [this 5 second sign up on our weekly mailing list](), and visit [Our Kindle Author Page]() to see other recently published Kindle titles.

We make these books for you and always want to know our readers' opinions, so we encourage you to leave reviews and look forward to publishing new and exciting titles each week.

Introduction

Bernard Gagnon's picture of Krak des Chevaliers, a Crusader castle in modern Syria

Crusader Castles

A series of mountain chains frame the Levantine coast, growing in height as they approach modern-day Lebanon. These provided a natural defense along the important coast, and the few passes through these mountain ranges were the focal points of movement and communication. For this reason, these locations were where many crusader castles were erected. Bristling with fortifications, these impressive structures were occupied by orders of knights that came to the Holy Land with the Pope's blessing, and who have gained a most romantic status over history. These Crusaders were called al-Faranj ("Franks") by the Arabs in the Holy Land, reflecting the French origins of many of the knights, even though the knights, soldiers, and pilgrims came to the Holy Land from all over Europe, and in particular from southern Italy, Germany, and England.

For the men who built and manned these castles, they were much more than buildings surrounded by stone walls or wooden palisades. They were also more than a headquarters for knights and their armies during battle, or a storehouse for goods in the remoteness of the Levant. These castles were the central focal point for those who held them and those trying to conquer them, and it would not be an exaggeration to claim that castles were the nexus for much activity and conflict within the Holy Lands.

At the same time, the castles were filled with the hustle and bustle of activity caused by a wide range of actors even in times of relative peace and stability. Men-at-arms were the soldiers who manned the castle, protected the borders of the Crusader States, and followed the orders of their noble knight lords, but the castles also served as a gathering place for skilled craftsmen such as blacksmiths, potters, stone masons, bakers, carpenters, and the like. Many served as religious centers in their own right, containing at least one chapel of either Christian or Muslim faith.

The Muslim efforts to reclaim and rule the Levant were just as important and interesting as those of the Crusaders. Initially led by the atabegs of Aleppo, and later by the renowned Saladin (known also as Salah Ed-Din), various Muslim forces took and retook the Holy City of Jerusalem. The cycle of conflicts between the Crusader states and the Muslim armies was disrupted in 1260 CE when the Mongols, having roved without obstruction across Eurasia, invaded the region with the support of the Armenians and some of the Crusader States. However, they were eventually defeated by the mighty Mamelukes of Egypt, who in turn focused their attention on consolidating their control over the Near East and eradicating the European presence in the region. Finally, in 1302 CE the Mamelukes conquered the last Crusader stronghold at Arwad, leaving one last remaining Crusader state - the Kingdom of Cyprus, which held out until it was invaded by the Ottomans in 1571 CE.

Crusader Castles: The History of the Medieval Castles Built in the Holy Lands during the Crusades examines the construction of the castles, daily life inside of them, and the fighting over them during the Crusades. Along with pictures of important people, places, and events, you will learn about Crusader castles like never before.

Crusader Castles: The History of the Medieval Castles Built in the Holy Lands during the Crusades

About Charles River Editors

Introduction

   Chapter 1: Building Castles in Peace and War

   Chapter 2: The Castles' Features

   Chapter 3: The Castles of the First Crusade

   Chapter 4: The Castles and Crusades of the 12th Century

   Chapter 5: The Decline of Crusader Castles in the 13th Century

   Online Resources

   Bibliography

Free Books by Charles River Editors

Discounted Books by Charles River Editors

Chapter 1: Building Castles in Peace and War

Before understanding the ins and outs of castle design, it is important to know who exactly was involved in their use in the Holy Land. During the time of the Crusades much of Europe operated under the feudal system, and this came with the knights who traveled to the Levant from the 11th century onwards. This system had a strictly stratified classification of authority and status, most generally between the chivalric nobility, the Christian church, and the ordinary peasants or serfs. At the top of it all was the royal family. Members of this group who were in the Holy Land could trace a direct family relationship to the ruling monarch in Europe, or may even be the monarch themselves, as in the case of Richard the Lionheart of England. In any feudal culture, members of this class were the absolute upper crust. Everyone – even the most powerful members of the nobility – was expected to swear fealty to the royal family and to their king in particular.[1]

The nobility were second in status only to the royal family, though in practice it was the nobles who were perhaps the most powerful of the classes. The nobility was made up of knights and barons who had been given a grant of land to administer, and a title stating as such. In some cases, they had earned the land themselves through wealth, power, or service to their king. In other situations the land may have been awarded to one of their ancestors and they had inherited the title and responsibilities which come with such an estate, as frequently happened during the later Crusades. Members of this class were endowed by their own lord with land of their own and a castle from which to dwell and protect the territory.[2] In return, they had to swear loyalty to their benefactor and the king, and vow to serve his interests in their daily lives. As such, they often paid a portion of their own incomes to him as a measure of their respect and gratitude, and in the frequent times of war in the Holy Land, they were expected to come promptly to the aid of their lord. It was therefore their responsibility to see to it that affairs in their lands were kept orderly, that the soldiers they commanded were well-trained and ready for war, and that all taxes and revenues due to the kingdom were collected in a timely manner.

As a rule, the king was replaced by his first born male child when he died. When there was no such heir, then a pre-established pecking order existed to decide who had a claim to the throne. In the event that no clear successor existed, the nobility would step in to select which member of the royal family would become the new king. In the event that a great disaster was to decimate the royal house, the successor to the throne would certainly come from the class of the nobility. In such cases, a great deal of political manipulation and deal-making would occur, and the means by which such an individual came to power could be very controversial. Political power struggles erupted whenever the throne of the Crusader states was left unclaimed, and would have had many important consequences.

---
[1] Nicolle, D. (2004) *Crusader Castles in the Holy Land 1097-1192*. Illinois: Osprey Publishing Ltd.
[2] Nicolle, 2004

The Crusaders and their lords recognized the absolute importance of the Church and the Holy Land. Members of the Christian – and most often the Catholic – church would be consulted on many important social and political issues. For their part, churches promoted a belief in the divine right of kings – a policy that reflected the belief that any king (or emperor) is himself a vassal who holds his own territory and legitimacy through the grace of God. This was generally accepted and supported by the royal family, not only because contemporary faith in the word of the Church was strong in general, but also because it bestowed upon the king and his actions a sense of divine guidance. This relationship between the church and the royal line is of key importance for understanding the Crusades, because it was due to this belief that many nations went to war with the apparent blessing of God, and even under His instructions.

To provide for the lord of the castle, his retinue of knights and soldiers, and for the servants and skilled artisans employed by him, a castle must also be thought to include the land that is farmed by the local peasants and the transport routes by which other vital supplies were brought by land and sea. Even the mightiest lord depended, in the long run, on the support of his serfs and supply of tithes from them. These are the people who tended the farms, worked the quarries, and who unfortunately most often found themselves in the middle of two warring faiths during the military campaigns. Although they are often relegated to the background of the feudal social order, and despite their histories remaining almost completely silenced by time, their importance in the Crusades should be recognized.

When the crusaders trekked east, they needed bases of operations from which to work, and that's how castles became so crucial. The castle's role was to be positioned on the ideal plot of land, in some strategically important area of the realm, and plant the foundations of the European or Muslim claim to the Holy Land through its sheer presence and indomitability. They were designed to be impenetrable thanks a complex of towers, bridges, and barriers built to protect it, but there were a number of vexing obstacles that had to be hurdled before such castles could be constructed.

The most obvious problem was how to acquire enough revenue and resources to build the castle.[3] In the time of the Crusades, castles were very expensive to build. A simple earth and timbre motte-and-bailey castle in continental Europe could cost huge amounts, and this cost would have multiplied in the war-torn Levant, where large stone castles were the preferred type.[4] The Crusaders also had to determine how they would come into possession of the land on which they wished to build – by royal instructions, payment of valuable goods, violent takeover, or some other means. Castles also required a great commitment of time and resources, not only for their initial construction but for any modifications and upkeep the fortresses required during their

---

[3] Kennedy, H. (1994) *Crusader Castles*. Cambridge: Cambridge University Press
[4] Nicolle, 2004

prolonged use.

Although these needs may sound enormous, this aspect of the castle construction was one of the easier tests to overcome before the castle was finished. Among the most daunting was the castle design itself, in terms of the size it should be, the defensive features it should possess, and how its residents would be accommodated and be able to survive there in times of both peace and war. These and other important aspects had to be decided upon during the earliest stages of occupying a castle; after all, the last thing that a Crusader force could afford was to have no well within the courtyard when coming under siege by Muslim armies. Castles therefore evolved throughout the Crusades in line with the weapons, siege technology, and tactics used against them.

Studying and making full use of the landscape were of vital importance for the construction and use of castles. The designer of the forts had to take into account the climate in which work was done, the terrain which workers had to deal with, the vegetation on the site, and the availability of resources. In addition to the complexity of organizing a large construction project – in what often was a remote location and difficult terrain – the castle designers thought of ways by which landscape features and topography might be worked to their advantage. For example, many castles were built upon the top of a scarp – a steep slope on the inner side of a ditch or ravine.

Communication was also of key importance for military affairs, and the disruption of communication networks during sieges was a problem faced by many such citadels. Thus, the designers of the castles responded in a number of interesting ways. For example, the strategically important castles of Krak des Chevaliers and Château de Margat could communicate with one another by way of an ingenious system of smoke signals and mirrors along the mountain ranges that led across the Levant, via the smaller Knights Templar castle of Chastel-Blanc.[5]

---

[5] Kennedy, 1994

An early 20th century picture of Chastel-Blanc

Castle design was often a modular process. For example, many simple fortresses consisted of little more than four round towers linked by a solid stone wall, with a basic gatehouse set in the center of one wall to allow entrance to the castle, all set upon an earthen motte. The bailey (or inner courtyard) would have included exercise and training areas, storerooms, and stables. Such a castle could be built by a relatively unskilled workforce.

From this basic layout of the structure, gradually more complex additions might be made over time, especially in response to potential exploitations of the defenses that had been identified when under siege.[6] However, better-trained laborers, more complicated construction engines (such as the treadwheel crane), taller wooden scaffolding, and greater access to the necessary resources would have been required as castles got more complex. It was for this reason that many castles were located close to the quarries from which the stone used in their construction was gathered.

---

[6] Nicolle, 2004

Great variation can be identified in the castles of the Crusades, reflecting the different backgrounds of those involved in their design and construction. Some castles were built of ashlar, squared blocks of smooth stone that had been neatly chiseled into shape. Others were rusticated, with the faces of the stones in the wall left rough, which was believed to provide better protection against bombardment by siege weapons. Archways are one revealing example, which varied between rounded, double-centered, or of the lancet style, sharply pointed in the shape of an acute triangle.[7]

What is left to be studied today is almost always only the stone remains of the castles, but most of them would have had extensive timber structures built around the complex. Sturdy wooden palisades may have existed around the castles that have not remained today – indeed, there is evidence that such wooden fences would have been erected to enclose the site when the stone castle was being built. Hoarding was common – wooden stories added atop the stone castle walls or keep. These included brattices (timber towers or projecting wooden galleries) and machicolations (wooden projecting balconies on brackets which would have been suspended from the tops of outer walls, with holes in their floor to be used to drop rocks and missiles upon the attackers below).

It was during the Crusades that many innovations were made in castle design, and this influenced the design of fortresses for many centuries afterwards.[8] There were three basic castle designs that existed at the time of the Crusades, which included the motte-and-bailey, the curtain wall type, and the concentric castle. Until the mid-13th century almost all of the castles built in Europe were of the motte-and-bailey type, a defense system based on an uncoordinated complex of walls and towers that aimed to wear down any attackers and provide the defender with many opportunities to strike back. They would also rely strongly on the impregnability of the central keep. However, this rarely worked as planned, and the attacker more often than not simply tackled each wall separately, reduced it to rubble and then moved on to the next barrier.

In the Levant, designers of castles shifted away from assuming that the central keep and bailey walls would be impregnable. They were increasingly aware that it was better to maintain a distance between the core of the citadel and the attacking force, and that it was wisest to keep the invaders from breaching the outermost wall – which would otherwise allow them in to ravage and plunder the many buildings and storage houses on the inside of the outer bailey that were vital for the defending force's survival during a prolonged siege.[9] Thus, the concentric form of castles was perfected during the Crusades, a design that enabled defenders to protect the castle walls from all angles – including from within.[10]

---

[7] Nicolle, 2004
[8] Fedden, R. (1970) "The Castles of the Crusaders." *Saudi ARAMCO World*, 21:3.
[9] Nicolle, 2004

The greatest period in castle development occurred during the last days of the 13th century and the beginning of the 14th century with the advancement of the concentric castle.[11] Such castles consisted of a number of circuit walls and towers, usually quadrangular in plan, surrounded by another lower wall with its own flanking towers. The area between these two walls, usually only a few tens of feet apart, was divided by a number of short cross walls that segmented the tight inner courtyard. Therefore, if any force penetrated the first wall, they would be confined to a small specific area and immediately confronted with a secondary defensive wall. The area in the confined space became the most dreaded area of any invading force, since almost all of the initial troops into this small area would be decimated by archers and falling stones from the higher inner wall.

It is impossible to approach a comprehensive study of the Crusader castles without also stressing the important role of Muslim citadels and castle design in the Levant. It was Muslim fortresses that the Crusaders encountered when they first arrived, and the Arab armies were extremely active in designing new castle features in response to the Crusaders' siege technologies. Beginning in the late 12th century, the Ayyubids engaged in a number of castle building projects across the Levant, including Aleppo, Damascus, Bosra, and Baalkbek. The frequent exchange of castles between the Crusaders and their foes enabled a melting pot of innovations with regards to castle design, as elements from European castle architecture influenced that of the Muslim forts, and vice versa.

Chapter 2: The Castles' Features

Castles were designed to make it as difficult as possible for invaders to move, fight, and survive outside and within their walls, and with that in mind, military architects, particularly those working during the Crusades, proved to have fertile (and often merciless) imaginations. Among their innovations were such things as "killing passages," murder holes, spiral staircases, spikes, and steep steps. Most castles had arrow slits or "loopholes" facing the outside - narrow vertical slits cut into a wall through which arrows could be fired from the inside while also protecting the archer from external return fire. Many also had them on the inner keep, facing the bailey so as to bombard anyone who managed to penetrate the outer walls.

A common design was the double gate or "killing passage." Once attackers had broken down a door or gate, they found themselves in a high-walled passage where the only exits were the gate through which they had just entered and an equally reinforced gate at the far end of the anteroom. However, set into the walls of the passage were many arrow slits, from which the totally protected defenders could fire upon the invaders with bows and crossbows. Further

---

[10] Nicolle, D. (2005) *Crusader Castles in the Holy Land 1192–1302*. Illinois: Osprey Publishing Ltd.
[11] Kennedy, 1994

damage was caused by so-called "murder holes" installed in the killing passage. Holes set into the ceiling would be used to drop arrows, rocks, boiling water, and possibly hot oil onto attackers trapped beneath. The attackers would be forced to either retreat or attempt to breach the second gate, all the while suffering massive losses from the withering crossfire from the sides and above.

Even such a simple thing as a staircase was turned into an obstacle for the attacker and a benefit for the defender. People would expect that each step in a flight of stairs would be of about the same height, but a common feature of many Crusader castles was the use of steep "trip steps": unexpectedly high steps that attackers would stumble upon if they were rushing up or down a staircase. Furthermore, the vast majority of spiral staircases—even those built today—form a clockwise helix, meaning that when one is climbing the stairs, they must turn right. This convention developed during the Crusades from a novel design decision made by castle architects. Being aware that soldiers were right-handed, and also conscious that most invaders would have to fight their way up a staircase, they developed the clockwise staircase. This meant that right-handed warriors attacking the castle (from below) would find that their sword swings were hampered by walls of the spiral, whereas the defenders above would have no such hindrance. Finally, many staircases used for external features – such as to access the outer walls or the keep – were built out of timber posts. This meant that they could be dismantled quickly or destroyed if the castle was threatened.

Robbie Gal's picture of the ruins of Monfort Castle in modern Israel

There were towers built in many different shapes and sizes in the Crusader states, from temporary timber brattices to strong stone keeps, otherwise known as donjons. Large, circular, and squat drum towers were built into the walls of concentric castles, their rounded shape providing an ideal means by which all areas of the external wall could be defended. Large towers on the curtain wall or on the middle of the outside wall were known as bastions, whilst numerous smaller rounded or polygonal turrets would have served as lookouts from the tallest points in the castle complex.

One of the most important contemporary advancements in castle design and fortification was the use of the flanking tower, which first began to appear in the late 12th and early 13th centuries in southern Europe and the Levant. Before this time, square towers had been set flush with the outer bailey wall, but the Crusader castle designers extended their towers outward, away from the rest of the wall. In doing so, defenders were able to fire from arrow slits on the sides of the towers along the length of the castle's curtain wall to the base of the tower on the opposite side. Furthermore, the earliest flanking towers were three-sided, with their backs open to the inner bailey, so that in the event the tower was captured by the invading force, they would prove of little worth (though as time went by, the flanking towers became square and protected on all sides). The advancements in the ability to make circular keeps also came to apply to the construction of flanking towers, and by the close of the 13th century most new flanking towers were cylindrical.

Rounded towers were most popular in the strongest and most famous Crusader castles. Their form provided a better defense against certain siege methods used by attackers, such as screws and sappers. As a rule, they tended to be somewhat smaller on the inside than their square counterparts, and they made use of less stone, which meant they also cost somewhat less to build.[12] The technology required to build such rounded structures, however, may not always have be available to the castle designer in the Holy Land. As noted earlier, many of the locations chosen to build castles were done so for their remoteness and difficulty of terrain, and it would therefore have been more difficult to assemble the engines required to build round towers. Although less sturdy and somewhat more expensive to make, in such cases square towers were easier to build than round ones.[13] For this reason they are somewhat more commonly found in the former Crusader states, even if they were admittedly weaker to some degree than their rounded counterpart.

Ditches were used in castle defense to make the land which attackers must cross uneven and dangerous. While giving their attention to getting past a ditch or other obstacle, attackers would have been far more vulnerable to defensive missile fire. Some of these trenches were filled with water (and could then be called a "moat"), though this was rare in the Levant, where a lack of water supply was a frequent problem. Depending on the depth of the surrounding ditch, castles would often have a flat space known as a "berm" in between the base of the curtain wall and the inner edge of the moat or trench. This level area was often the focal point of attackers who could use the space for their siege engines. For this reason, many castle walls and towers in the Holy Land display a sharply sloping base on the exterior face known as a "talus" or "batter," which was designed to prevent tunneling from underneath and prevent siege engines from being brought fully up to the walls. They would also cause stones dropped from above by the defenders to shatter upon impact, the shrapnel of which would cause great damage to any attacking infantry below. Furthermore, walls were strengthened with solid stone buttresses, sloping wall projections that gradually receded into the structure as it ascended from its wide base which provided extra support against siege engines.[14]

---

[12] Nicolle, 2004
[13] Nicolle, 2004
[14] Ellenblum, R. (2001) "Frankish and Muslim Siege Warfare and the Construction of Frankish Concentric Castles." In M. Balard (*ed.*) *Die Gesta per Francos*. Aldershot

Jean Dunston's picture of Kyrenia Castle near Girne in Cyprus

Berthold Werner's picture of Kerak in modern Jordan

The walls were arguably the most important feature of Crusader castles. They provided the first line of defense before the keep, and in many cases they were so well designed that the defending force could make full use of the amenities of the bailey throughout the siege (most important of which was usually the castle's water supply). The most important wall was therefore the "curtain wall" that was usually positioned in between two towers and surrounded the bailey. Because of their importance, numerous innovations were made in the design of castle walls during the Crusades to improve their defensive capabilities. For example, "joggled" masonry was used in some forts, by which joints were overlapped and sometimes strengthened with metal bands to improve their integrity.

The main improvements to the fortified walls were measures that provided cover for archers, modified battlements to withstand siege engines, and wide walkways that gave free movement to large numbers of troops and knights on the increasingly wide walls and towers. There still existed the major problem of siege weapons and sappers – attacking soldiers who would mine beneath walls either to provide access to the bailey or to cause the wall to sag and weaken – at the base of the bailey. The only solution to keeping the attackers away from the bailey wall was to prevent the attackers from getting close enough in the first place. This was solved by the implementation of a number of features in the castle walls that enabled the full scale bombardment of warriors at the base of the fortification. The walls were topped with an "allure," or walkway, which allowed defenders to move quickly around the castle perimeter and bombard the attackers, all while being protected from return fire by crenelated battlements (a narrow wall or parapet built along the outer edge of the wall with indentations or "embrasures" and raised sections known as "merlons" in between). This meant that the defender did not have to expose his body to attacking archers in an attempt to shoot invaders nearing the wall.

Another way to protect the wall from siege engines like the ram, pick, or screw was through the use of brattices and hoardings, which allowed missiles and stones to be dropped through slots in the floor – though they tended to be easy targets for return fire from catapults and ballista-like weapons.

The main entrance of early medieval castles was protected most frequently by a barbican set into the outer and curtain walls of the fortress. Barbicans were composed of two or more towers set some distance apart with a stone building linking their upper sections together. The space beneath the suspended building would either be left open or would house a gate secured by a heavy timber door-bolt set between two bar holes or a portcullis (a heavy timber or metal grill that could be raised or lowered from within the barbican or gatekeep – it would drop vertically from the ceiling, and in doing so could be used to block access or even to trap attackers within a confined space to be finished off).

During the 11th century and well into the later periods of the Crusades, the gatekeep was one of the most important aspects of castle design. A major step in the evolution of the castle, it was this structure that protected the entranceway into the castle. The gatekeep permitted the defenders of the castle to confront attackers before they reached the actual main gates leading into the bailey.

At the start of the Crusades, the gatekeep frequently consisted of two square towers on each side of the bailey wall. This was later replaced by four towers, two at each end of the entrance way, connected by a short stone wall that provided excellent protection and bottled up the enemy in the event that the gatekeep was breached. In essence, this later type of gatekeep was much like a barbican-style gateway that was set away from the castle walls but connected to them via a pair of strong stone walls.[15] Troops were able to move freely from one tower to another without fear of being struck by enemy artillery. Even if the outer barriers of the gatekeep were breached, the walls acted to create a "killing passage" that made the final assault on the gates even more difficult, as the floors and walls of the connecting structure had murder holes and embrasures through which attackers could be assaulted. Furthermore, the gatekeep allowed defenders to sally

---

[15] Nicolle, 2004

forth outside of the bailey to the "doorstep" of the castle to engage with the enemy, while still allowing them to quickly withdraw from the field of battle without endangering the fortress itself.

Throughout the 12th century the four towers were most frequently of a squared plan, but by the mid-13th century, these towers evolved into a rounded form. As the principle of the gatekeep design took hold in the Holy Land, additional defenses, called barbicans, were often built to add a further layer of protection to the castle entrance. The barbican acted as a miniature bailey, with walls extending at right angles from the gatekeep. Any attackers therefore had to pass through a very narrow cleft, from which artillery and archers from within the castle could bombard missiles down upon the intruders.[16] As time went by, these outer bailey walls took on their own stone towers, moats, ditches, and drawbridges to further strengthen the entranceway into the castle proper. Drawbridges were heavy timber platforms built to span between the gatekeep and the surrounding ditch, moat, or other landscape features, which could be raised when required to block an entrance.

Salim Darwiche's picture of Sidon Castle in modern Lebanon

---

[16] Nicolle, 2005

The castles of the Crusades contained a number of features that related more to their use in times of relative peace than of war, and archaeologists have managed to create a vividly detailed picture of daily life and its material context in a number of Crusader castles. The knowledge is so extensive that it is even known the occupants went to the toilet within spaces known as "garderobes," which were small latrines built into the castle walls – or even projecting out from them in a space known as a "bartizan" – from which human waste would be collected in a cesspit.[17]

> **Comment [PE]:** Are you talking about the "garderobes?"

Castles had to be secure spaces, even in times of peace, as they frequently held great wealth and expensive weaponry. For this reason, internal doors were made of thick and heavy timber boards hung on iron pintels that were solidly set into the stone door frame. They were frequently reinforced with iron bands and studs, making them increasingly difficult to break down with a battering ram or hatchets. These would have been locked with iron keys and complex locks.[18] Many of these were built around the edges of the bailey, or within the central keep.[19]

The lord of the castle lived within the solar or great chamber, which was usually the uppermost living room located above the great hall. The great hall, also known as the refectory, was the main meeting and dining area for the castle's residents and served also as the throne room in some cases. They would have been quite gloomy rooms, as medieval windows in the Holy Land were not large and very rarely glazed, though the spaces would have been warmed by tremendous fireplaces. Castles often had more than one kitchen, each of which were devoted to preparing different types of food. Throughout the earlier Crusades an open fire remained the only method of cooking food, but by the 13th century brick and mortar hearths were being installed in some castles.[20] There were also butteries, rooms from which wine (not butter) was dispensed.[21]

Castles also contained a number of structures with religious associations. Chapels, chancels, and private oratories could all be found in even the smallest of castles, some of them with recessed aumbries used to hold sacred vessels. The water supply was of key importance in the Holy Land, in times of both peace and war. For this reason wells and cisterns were almost always installed within the confines of the outer walls, and frequently even within the central keep.

---

[17] Molin, 1997
[18] Kennedy, 1994
[19] Molin, K. (1997) "The non-military functions of Crusader fortifications, 1187-circa 1380." *Journal of Medieval History*, 23. 367-388.
[20] Molin, 1997
[21] Kennedy, 1994

Chapter 3: The Castles of the First Crusade

In the mid-11th century, the Rum Seljuk occupation of Anatolia began (1071 – 1307 CE). These Turkish tribes occupied most of Asia Minor after defeating the Byzantine armies of Emperor Romanos IV at Manzikert in 1071 CE, and following this victory they gradually expanded westwards as far as Nicea and southwards towards Syria and Fatimid Egypt.[22] In 1076 CE the Seljuks conquered Jerusalem, pillaging the holy city and slaughtering its residents.[23]

Aside from a few pockets of resistance, like Christian Armenia and the Shi'ite Assassins, the Seljuk Empire dominated the region for a half-century. The height of the Empire's power came with the Battle of Manzikert in 1071, in which the bellicose Byzantine Emperor Romanos IV Diogenes (c.1030-72) was defeated and captured by Seljuq general Alp Arslan (1029-72) in eastern Anatolia. Romanos was treated well and later released, but he was deposed and died after being blinded (blinding being the favored way in Byzantine politics to get rid of a political rival without killing him, since a blind man could not be Emperor). Even though Arslan also died soon after, slain by an assassin, it was a turning point for the Byzantine Empire, which began a slow decline into military irrelevance thereafter. The situation for the Palestinian Christians under the Seljuqs remains unclear, due to a lack of direct evidence from the area in that period, but chroniclers like Michael the Syrian indicate that they were persecuted at least to some extent.

Even at its height, the Seljuk Empire lacked a strong infrastructure and existed in a state of perpetual warfare. Syria, in the Western Levant, was loosely organized into squabbling leaders distantly swearing allegiance to Baghdad and soon began to fall apart, while Palestine was contested by the Fatimids. In the wake of the empire's growing weakness, the Byzantine Emperor, Alexius Comnenus (1056-1118), saw an opportunity to regain some territory. He had hired Frankish mercenaries before, so he sent a letter to the Pope in Rome asking for more help. What was different was the Pope's reaction, which was quite startling. He called for something new – a crusade.

Whereas under the Fatimids relative peace existed between the Muslims and pilgrims from other faiths who traveled to Jerusalem, the Seljuk conquest of the city spurred the successor of Romanos IV, Emperor Alexios I, to request help from the other side of the schismatic Church: the Holy Roman Empire, centered in the Vatican City in Rome.[24]

At the time, an increasingly turbulent Western European society needed an outlet for its violence, as well as rapidly changing borders between Christians and Muslims in the

---

[22] Venning, T. (2015) *A Chronology of the Crusades*. London: Routledge
[23] Cahen, C. (1988) *The Seljukid Sultanate of Rum, 11th to 14th Centuries*. London: Longman
[24] Venning, 2015

Mediterranean and Western Asia. Viking attacks in the north and west and Muslim attacks in the south and east had put Europe into a siege mentality, and though trade continued (in contradiction to Henri Pirenne's famous thesis), European Christians became very wary of non-Christians, including Jews, while struggling to deal with a major contraction of territory.

The practicalities of seasonal weather usually meant that summer was the only time warfare could be fought, which was also (unfortunately) the busiest time of year for peasants and the riskiest in terms of losing their crops to pillaging and scorched earth policies by feuding knights. In addition, even the knights, some of them only Christian for a few generations, began to worry about the state of their own souls. Raised to fight and kill as their *raison d'être*, they also struggled with the pacifist rules of Christianity. Could one be a good Christian and still be a warrior?

Finally, there was the conflict between Church and State. This had not been a problem in previous centuries, when the Church had been weak in temporal terms and served largely as a moderating influence. The European states, in addition, were also weak and decentralized. But this began to change in the 11th century, when the Church began to gain temporal power and assert itself over secular bodies, and it led to a major conflict between the Papacy and the Holy Roman Empire (formerly allies) that was known as the Investiture Controversy, which lasted from 1075 until 1122. Pope Gregory VII (c.1015-85) became irritated at the common (and corrupting) practice of local nobility investing local clergy, hence the name of the controversy. Gregory believed in a centralized, less-worldly clergy that answered only to Rome – a separation of church and state, so to speak.

When the Byzantines sought help, just how much Pope Urban II was actually concerned about the Seljuks' occupation of the Holy Land is a subject of some debate among historians. Thomas Asbridge speculated that Urban hoped to reunite the Western and Eastern Churches, at that time still only recently divided, and he also asserted the crusade disrupted the peaceful relations between Islam and Christianity. Conversely, Thomas Madden believed that the crusade was motivated by genuine feeling and a real concern about imbalance between the two religions by the Seljuq invasions. Moshe Gil further argued that reports about the region generally show an increase in violence against religious minorities and pilgrims in the 11th century. Christopher Tyerman takes a middle view that both internal violence and reports of religious violence from the Holy Land were the main motivations, while Jonathan Riley-Smith leans toward economic motivations of territorial expansion. On balance, the state of constant civil war in the Levant appears to have left the Franks (Western Christians) genuinely concerned about increasing violence toward Christian pilgrims in Palestine and worried that Christians might eventually be unable to visit Jerusalem or even the Holy Land itself.

Depiction of Urban II

At the same time, however, it seems they were also motivated by concerns closer to home. Most crusades historians now agree that the crusades were motivated largely by idealism, with variations like economic pressures, a fear of the Islamic threat and Urban's desire to expand the power of the Latin Church. Still, there have been a few holdouts, like Steven Runciman, who argued that the crusaders were motivated by a sense of adventure and disagreed with near-contemporary William of Tyre's assertion that the crusade was a response to the Muslim threat in the Middle East. Joseph Prawer even argued that the crusaders were early models of European colonialism.

It is also not entirely clear how Urban came up with the idea of a crusade to the Holy Land. His predecessor Gregory had made a previous call in 1074, using the term, *"milites Christi"* (soldiers of Christ), but it had been largely ignored. It is possible that Urban had heard of the Muslim concept of jihad or holy war, and the concept of aggressive expansion through holy war was not at all unknown to Christians by that period.

However he conceived the idea, Urban decided to give a speech calling his audience to go on a crusade to the Holy Land, to win back Jerusalem and cleanse the Holy Land of the Muslim threat, using the Byzantine Emperor's letter as an excuse. Even still, it is unlikely he was aware that he would get the response that he did, for it was unprecedented. He had perhaps hoped at best to gain some mercenaries to send to the Byzantine emperor, a few donations, or perhaps even an small army.

That said, his speech was not spontaneous; he had planned it very carefully, maneuvering to bring in leaders of the crusade before announcing it. Urban spoke to a large number of people in Clermont, France on November 27, 1095. This was known as the Council of Clermont, and the subject was the letter from Alexius. After a brief exhortation against the fratricidal violence of the knights (Urban, himself, came from nobility), Urban related the news that the Seljuks had conquered Romania and were attacking Europe as far west as Greece. He painted a picture of Christianity in grave danger from this new, Turkish threat, even mentioning them separately from the Arabs as another group of enemies against Christians in the Middle East.

Depiction of Pope Urban II preaching the First Crusade at the Council of Clermont

As he spoke, his audience began to respond in an enthusiastic, even violent, manner. They wept and shouted and swore that they would leave right away for the Holy Land, proclaiming in Old French, "*Deus li volt!*" (God wills it!). Urban had brought with him red crosses of cloth for people to sew onto their clothes, which his assistant, Bishop Adhémar of Le Puy (who would later be appointed the papal legate of the crusade and die in 1098) handed out, but they quickly ran out of them. In a disquieting parody of the miracle of the loaves and fishes from the New Testament, people tore their own clothing and cut crosses out to hand around. Adhémar was the first to officially take the cross. Urban spent the rest of the year touring France and giving speeches to rally people to the cause.

The knights responded with special enthusiasm to Urban's promise of absolution, which was clearly Urban's intent. Here, finally, was the marriage of religious and secular that they had longed for. Here was a way for them to act as knights in a way that served God. It was a potent message for them and it is entirely possible that Urban had crafted it just for them. But they were hardly the only ones affected. Peasants were also inspired in great numbers and two armies quickly grew up – one a peasant army and one consisting of nobles with their entourages and small personal armies. The peasant army left first, a large, inchoate mob headed in a wandering path through Eastern Europe for the Holy Land.

The official date for the crusade was fixed by Urban for August 15, 1096, but the peasant army had already left months before, in early March. Known as the "People's Crusade," a large rabble of pious peasants marched to the Holy Land, but they were quickly defeated during their first attack at Nicea.[25] They would be followed in May 1097 by an army of professionally trained soldiers led by noble knights, who captured Nicea from the Seljuks.

When a crusader army of Western European Franks took Jerusalem by storm on July 15, 1099, it was one of the more unexpected conquests in history. Everything seemed to be against them for the previous three years of they crusade, right up to the final siege, and yet they finally prevailed. And when they did, they massacred most, if not all, of the population, before establishing a Christian realm in a region that had been taken over by the Muslims in 634.

Even today, the First Crusade remains a difficult and polarizing event to debate, even among modern historians. For some, the crusaders were heroes and saints, and for others they were devils who disrupted the peaceful local sects of Muslims, Jews, and Christians, establishing an alien colony that heralded modern European imperialism. To serve the needs of whatever story they want to tell, some historians will begin their tale at some convenient point in history that makes one side look good. In fact, the First Crusade is also a signal example of why it is unwise to choose sides in history, because neither side was correct and the situation was highly complex.

Regardless, it was during the First Crusade that the major states and kingdoms of the Holy Land were established. The Crusaders established their first state in the Holy Land via the County of Edessa, centered on Edessa (modern day Sanliurfa).[26] They then besieged and captured Antioch, and Bohemond of Taranto became the first ruler of the Principality of Antioch.[27] A week after taking Jerusalem in 1099, the crusaders crowned Godfrey of Bouillon as the first king of the Latin Kingdom of Jerusalem. Soon afterwards, Raymond of Toulouse besieged and

---

[25] Venning, 2015
[26] Venning, 2015
[27] Asbridge, T. (2000) *The Creation of the principality of Antioch.* Woodbridge: Boydell and Brewer

seized the coastal city of Tripoli, which became the center of the County of Tripoli in 1109 CE.[28] This last Crusader state was relatively minor compared to the others, and it operated as a vassal to the Kingdom of Jerusalem until it eventually became assimilated by the Principality of Antioch.[29]

---

[28] The fifth, and final, Crusader state was the Kingdom of Cyprus, which was founded during the Third Crusade after the island – owned by the Byzantines – was conquered by King Richard the Lionheart in 1191 CE.
[29] Asbridge, 2000

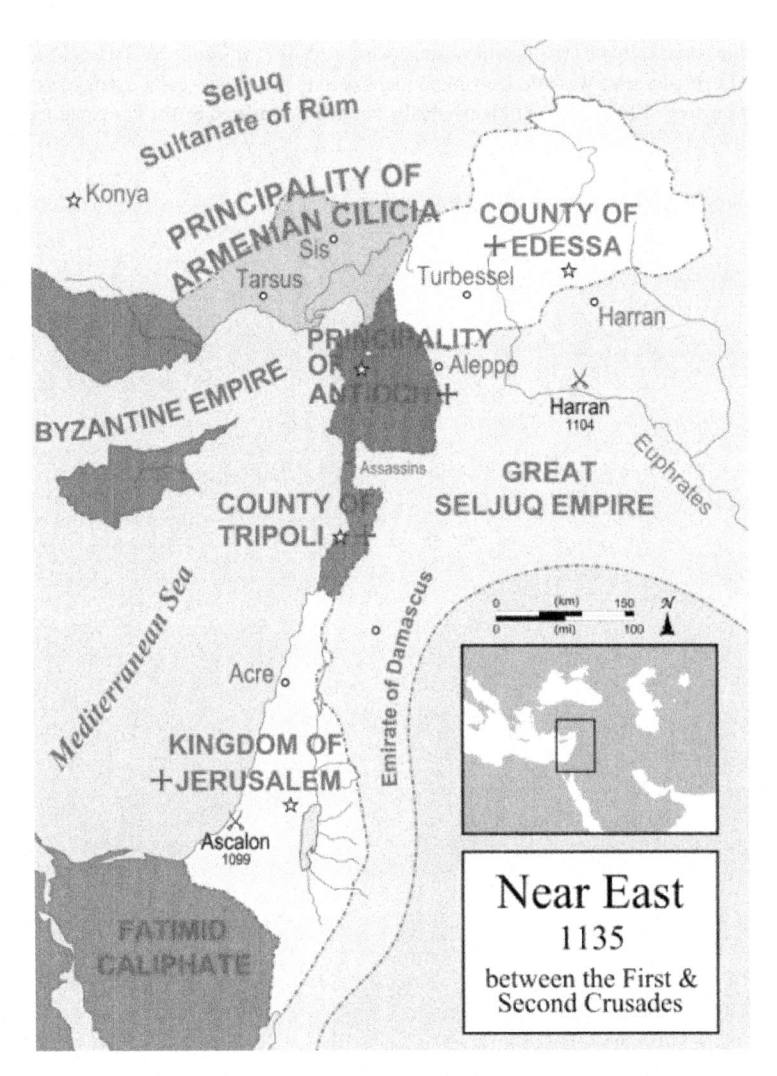

A map of the Crusader states between the first two crusades

Naturally, Jerusalem was at the center of the Crusades, a city of central importance to three of the world's largest faiths and a site battled over for millennia. The city was particularly dependent on the network of fortified castles surrounding it, in particular those along its eastern border and the Mediterranean – depending on the perspective of who held the Holy City. Evidence of a fortification in the area exists from at least the 2nd century BCE. The site itself has had a wide array of civilizations and cultures making use of the location as a fortress, including the Hasmoneans, Herodians, the Romans, Christians, Muslims, Mamelukes, and Ottomans.

The Tower of David was the main castle of the city during the Crusades.[30] The site acquired its name from the Byzantines in the 5th century CE, who maintained that it was once the palace of King David.[31] When the Muslim Arabs conquered the city in 638, they restored the ancient towers from the Roman and pre-Roman periods, and it became one of the mightiest structures in the Levant for the next 300 years.[32] It withstood the attempted invasion by the European Crusaders in 1099 CE, though eventually the inhabitants agreed to surrender in order to save the residents of the city.

Under Crusader control a number of modifications were made to the castle. A large tower was erected atop the keep, in order to provide a better overview of the surrounding landscape, and in particular of the road to Jaffa along which many pilgrims were travelling. They also excavated a deep ditch around the citadel.[33]

---

[30] Murphy-O'Connor, J. (2008) *The Holy Land: An Oxford Archaeological Guide from Earliest Times to 1700*. Oxford: Oxford University Press
[31] Angold, M. (1984) *The Byzantine Empire 1025–1204: a Political History*. London: Longman
[32] Chevedden, P.E. (1999) "Fortification and the Development of Defensive Planning in the Latin East." In D. Kagay and L.J.A. Villalon (*eds.*) *The Circle of War in the Middle Ages*. Woodbridge
[33] Cohen, A. (1989) "The Walls of Jerusalem." In C.E. Bosworth (*ed.*) *Essays in Honor of Bernard Lewis; The Islamic World from Classical to Modern Times*. Princeton: Princeton University Press

The Tower of David and the city walls

In 1187 Saladin successfully captured Jerusalem, including the Tower of David. Much of the castle was destroyed in 1239 by the Ayyubid emir of Karak, An-Nasir Dawud, and the destruction was completed by the Mamelukes during their invasion in 1260.[34] However, it was subsequently rebuilt in 1310 by the Mameluke sultan Al-Nasir Muhammad ibn Qalawun.[35]

Known today as Shawbak, Montreal Castle was founded by Baldwin I, first King of Jerusalem (r. 1100 – 1118) in 1115 during his early expansionist campaigns towards the Dead Sea in the region known to the Crusaders as Oultrejourdain (present-day Jordan). The citadel was positioned atop a tall mountain on the range of Moab, rising from the flat plateau of Edom. It was located in such a way as to take advantage of the commercial potential of the main caravan route passing between Damascus, Egypt, and the holy places of the Arabian Peninsula and of the

---

[34] Pringle, D. (1995) "Town Defenses in the Crusader Kingdom of Jerusalem." In Corfis, I.A. and Wolfe, M. (*eds.*) *The Medieval City under Siege.* Woodbridge
[35] Murphy-O'Connor, 2008

Hijaz.[36]

Bernard Gagnon's picture of the ruins of the castle

---

[36] Kennedy, 1994

A close look at one of the castle's towers

Although the ruins seen today are those that remain from the much later Mameluke occupation of the fortress, Baldwin's early castle consisted of triple walls and a particularly massive curtain wall. The bailey contained two chapels. The castle was well-defended by the natural features of the landscape. It stood upon an isolated, steeply sloping craggy hill, leaving no angle by which siege engines might be able to approach the walls. The surrounding lowlands were well-watered meaning that it had a fertile hinterland from which to draw supplies. However, water supply within the lofty fortress remained a key problem, which the Crusaders solved by constructing a spiraled staircase of three hundred and sixty five steps that led down within the hill to a number of cisterns constructed in the depths of the earth.[37] This provided the occupants with an unlimited supply of fresh, spring-fed water in times of siege.

Saladin laid siege to Montreal at the same time as Kerak, and though Kerak surrendered to the Arab armies in 1188, Montreal's defenders held out for so long that they ended up going blind due to the lack of salt in their diet. They initially refused all offers from Saladin to provide them with money and safe passage to Christian lands, but they eventually surrendered in 1189.

Also known as *Château de Margat* and *Qalaat al Marqab* ("Castle of the Watchtower"), Marqab was one of the most important fortresses in the County of Tripoli due to its location near the coast and on the border of the Principality of Antioch. It is situated near present-day Baniyas in Syria in the ancient Crusader Principality of Antioch, and served as a major stronghold for both the Knights Hospitallers and Knights Templar.

The first fortress here was built by local Muslim emirs in 1062, and it served as a bastion against the Principality of Antioch during and after the First Crusade. However, after the Battle of Harran in 1104, Marqab was captured from the Muslims by the Byzantines, and shortly afterwards Tancred, Prince of Galilee and regent of Antioch, conquered it and incorporated it into the Principality of Antioch.[38] Reynald II Mazoir of Antioch later ruled the castle as the vassal Count of Tripoli, and ownership of the fort was transferred to the Order of the Knights of St. John in 1186 (along with Krak des Chevaliers which protected the territory's eastern borders; see below).

The castle that the Hospitallers built was triangular in shape, though with some elements of a concentric plan. It was protected on one side by the steeply sloping and deep ravine of the extinct volcano upon which it was built, more than 360 meters above sea level.[39] The remaining two

---

[37] Kennedy, 1994
[38] "Margat Castle (or Marquab Castle): Ruined Crusader Castle in Syria." *Castles and Manor Houses*. (http://www.castlesandmanorhouses.com/page.php?key=Margat%20Castle%20(or%20Marquab%20Castle))
[39] "Margat Castle (or Marquab Castle): Ruined Crusader Castle in Syria." *Castles and Manor Houses*. (http://www.castlesandmanorhouses.com/page.php?key=Margat%20Castle%20(or%20Marquab%20Castle))

sides had a double layer of massive and high curtain walls joining at a central round tower.[40] Entrance was via a passageway that bent at right angles as it led to the inner courtyard, defended on either side by arrow slits and with murder holes from above. Within their confines was the fortified keep, the center of the fortress. These structures were made of the same deep black basalt as the rocky escarpment that the castle was built upon.[41] Beautifully worked decorative embellishments were integrated around the doorways of the donjon and chapel in limestone. Within the outer walls was a large central courtyard. In addition to the main keep, in which the Knights Hospitallers resided in the upper stories, there was a large chapel, a knight's hall used for meetings and feasts, armories, and storerooms. A well provided water in times of a siege.

The castle was first besieged in 1188 by Saladin. Shortly after he conquered Jerusalem, the Ayyubid leader sought to take control of the fortress, which defended the main communications and travel route between Tripoli and Latakia. However, the Knights Hospitallers managed to endure the siege, and the castle continued to serve as one of the most important locations in the region. It was here that Richard the Lionheart sent the defeated Isaac Comnenus of Cyprus to be imprisoned after conquering the Kingdom of Cyprus during the Third Crusade, and in 1240 it served as the headquarters of the Bishop of nearby Valenia.[42]

The castle remained unconquerable even when it was attacked in 1271 by the prodigious Mameluke sultan Baibars, who had a short time before managed to overcome the defenses at Krak des Chevaliers. Eventually, however, the fortress at Marqab met its match when the castle was besieged by Sultan Qalawun in 1285. Qalawun had massive siege engines assembled, which bombarded the castle walls, and sent sappers to lay mines underneath their foundations. Seeing the damage that was being applied, and realizing that the castle would not be able to sustain much more, the Hospitallers reached a peace agreement with Qalawun by which they would be allowed to travel safely to Tortosa in exchange for surrendering the castle. It was from Marqab that Qalawun later assembled the Mameluke army before their final invasion of Tripoli in 1289.

---

[40] Nicolle, 2005
[40] Venning, 2015
[41] Nicolle, 2005
[42] Petre, 2010

Chapter 4: The Castles and Crusades of the 12th Century

The success of the First Crusade shaped the rest of the Middle Ages, including culture, politics, religion, technology, and development of chivalry and knightly piety, and \ what amounted to Europe's earliest colonial ventures into the Near East.[43] However, less than a century later, in 1169 Saladin conquered Egypt and established the Ayyubid dynasty soon after. He subsequently embarked on a number of campaigns to expand his territory northwards into the Levant, and in particular focused his attention on the Muslim emirates of Syria.

By the mid-1170s Saladin was ready for his major goal: to reconquer Jerusalem from the Crusaders of the First Crusade. In 1177 he initiated his campaign into the Kingdom of Jerusalem from the south. It was the loss of Edessa to the Muslim armies that sparked Europeans to embark on the Second Crusade, launched in the 1140s by two of the most heroic figures of the 12th century: Louis VII of France and Conrad, the Emperor-elect of Germany.[44] Saladin was defeated by King Baldwin IV of Jerusalem, who was famed for the heroic deeds he achieved despite suffering severely from leprosy, a condition that killed him in 1185 at the young age of 24. He was a skilled warrior and leader, and he defeated Saladin on a number of occasions after coming of age in 1177. However, in 1179 it was Saladin who was victorious over the Crusaders, this time at the Battle of Marj Ayyun.

Fighting between the two dominions continued until 1180, when Saladin made a tentative peace with King Baldwin of Jerusalem and Raymond III of Tripoli. However, this lasted for only two years, when Reynald of Châtillon – ruler of Kerak – violated the treaty and provoked Saladin to war after attacking Muslim caravans traveling through Transjordan.

From the mid-12th century onwards, two military orders became particularly important in the Holy Land in general, and with regards to castle building and use in particular. These were the Hospitallers, also known as the Order of the Knights of St. John, and the Knights Templar. Throughout the 13th century these two orders played a key role in the defense of the Crusader States. It was through their patronage and labor – and numerous sacrifices in battle – that castles were erected and defended at the most important border crossings and strategic locations.

Known also as *Crac des Moabites*, Kerak Castle[45] was a massive fortress located in the Crusader territory of Oultrejordain (Transjordan). It was one of the largest castles to have ever been built in the Holy Lands. The earliest fortress was constructed here in the 1140s, under the

---

[43] Venning, 2015
[44] Venning, 2015
[45] Not to be confused with Krak des Chevaliers

instructions of Paganus, a manservant of Fulk of Jerusalem and later lord of Oultrejordain. Kerak was the center of his dominion, serving as a key node along the land-based trade routes connecting Damascus to North Africa and the Arabian Peninsula, as well as to Central Asia.[46]

    The castle is protected by the steeply sloping spur upon which it is built, with two deep ditches on the northern and southern sides. The surrounding walls feature tall, projecting rectangular towers built of locally quarried white limestone. These served as the residential quarters of the approximately sixty knights who resided in the castle, and who commanded the men-at-arms within. It also featured upper and lower courtyards. On the western side of the bailey is the tremendous Hall of the Knights. The bailey had a chapel on its southern end and an interior northern wall on the opposite site that is exceptionally well-preserved to this day. It consisted of a series of two-story arched halls that were used as residential quarters on the upper floors, and stables or warehouses below. The galleries also had defensive functions, as archers could fire from the narrow windows to attackers below whilst being protected from return fire. The castle does not lack ornamentation, with richly carved stonework incorporated into the walls and framing doorways throughout the complex.[47]

---

[46] Pringle, D. and De Meulemeester, J. (2000) *The Castle of al-Karak*. Jordan: Namur
[47] Pringle and De Meulemeester, 2000

Bernard Gagnon's picture of the ruins of Kerak

Dennis Jarvis' picture of ornamentation on a wall

Daniel Case's picture of the interior of Kerak

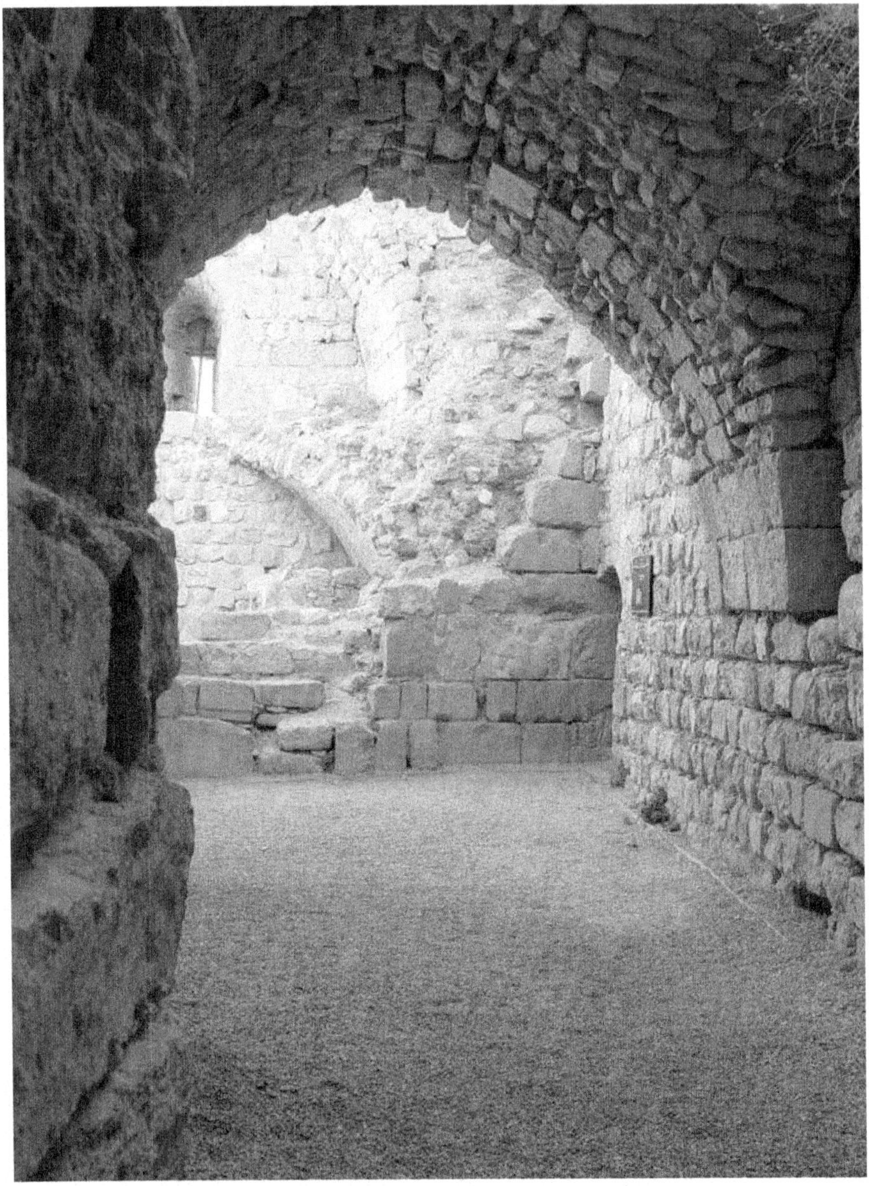

Steven Price's picture of an archway inside the castle

In 1176 the nobleman Reynald of Châtillon acquired Kerak through marriage. From this stronghold he engaged in a number of raids against Muslim trade caravans passing through Transjordan. Infuriated, Saladin proclaimed that the treaty formed with King Baldwin in 1180 was broken, and he besieged Kerak in 1183. The siege was eventually lifted after King Baldwin marched the army of Jerusalem to Kerak. After his victory at Hattin in 1187 Saladin once again attacked Kerak, and two years later managed to conquer it. The Mamelukes gained control of the castle later in the 13th century, and in 1263 Sultan Baibars added to those fortifications by building an enormous tower on the northwestern corner.[48]

Known also as Beauvoir ("Fair View"), the Frankish castle of Belvoir was located approximately 20 kilometers south of the Sea of Galilee and approximately 150 kilometers north of Jerusalem.[49] Belvoir was initially settled by a Frankish nobleman named Velos, who resided in the nearby fortified settlement of Tiberias. Ownership of the site transferred to Gilbert of Assailly, leader of the Hospitallers, who purchased it from Velos in 1168. Construction of the fortress began that same year atop a high and steeply sloping basalt plateau known as Naphtali, from which it had a strategically important view of the surrounding farmlands, an important bridge over the River Jordan, and the road linking the hills of Gilead and the Kingdom of Jerusalem. Because of its lofty position more than five hundred meters above the Jordan River Valley, it was described by contemporaries as being "set among the stars like an eagle's nest and abode of the moon", and it became one of the most important sites protecting the Holy Land's eastern borders.[50]

---

[48] Pringle and De Meulemeester, 2000
[49] The Hebrew name of the castle is Kochav Hayarden, meaning "Star of the Jordan", and under the Arabian Caliphates it was known as Kawkab al-Hawa, meaning "Star of the Winds"
[50] Kennedy, 1994

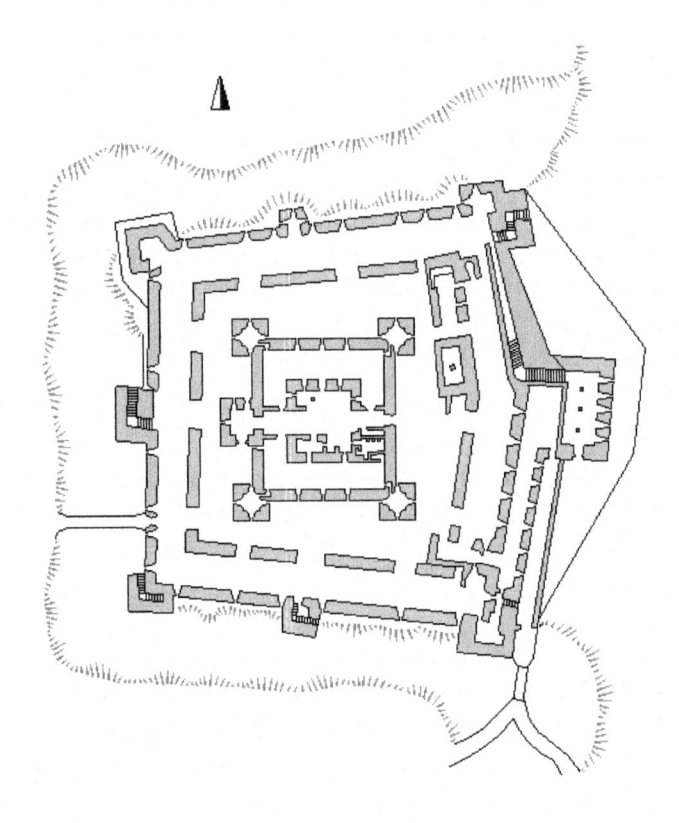

The layout of Belvoir Castle in modern Israel

The ruins of Belvoir Castle today

It took five years for the castle to be completed, with many hundreds of laborers brought in for the project. It had a symmetrical concentric plan,[51] with both an inner and an outer rectangular wall. The fortress was also surrounded by a deep, dry moat on the southern, western, and northern sides, and had an extremely steep slope leading to the main entrance on the south eastern side, all of which prevented siege engines from approaching the walls. The outer wall had formidable square towers constructed on each of the corners and smaller ones in between them on each side, whilst the inner keep had five similar towers, one on each corner and another on the western wall.[52] These towers had steeply sloping taluses at their bases, which prevented attackers from tunneling beneath the walls. With so many towers encircling the castle, all angles could be protected by archers who could fire through narrow holes on the crest.[53] A tremendous barbican protected the main entrance through the outer defenses to the southeast, whilst access to

---

[51] The castle might be the oldest that made use of a concentric ground plan; see Sire, H. J. A. (1994) *The Knights of Malta*. New Haven: Yale University Press

[52] Nicolle, 2004

[53] Further information, including detailed plans and photographs, can be found at "Belvoir Castle: Ruined Concentric Crusader Castle in Israel." *Castles and Manor Houses* (http://www.castlesandmanorhouses.com/p.php?key=Belvoir)

the inner fort was from the western edge – meaning that attackers would have to circle uphill along the surrounding paved courtyard whilst under heavy fire to even reach the fortified gateway to the keep.[54] The gates were secured by a heavy timber door lined with metal strips, which were secured from within by a wooden beam that slid between holes on either side. There was a smaller, secondary entrance through the outer wall from the west, across a drawbridge that covered the moat, which was 14 meters deep and 20 meters wide. Furthermore, there were sally ports into the moat accessible from the outer towers, yet these were secured from within and installed with extremely narrow and steep staircases – making them especially hard for attackers to use even if they gained access.[55]

The masonry of these fortifications was assembled in a most ingenious manner, as joints between the basalt ashlar stones were filled with U-shaped metal strips, increasing their durability. Within the walls were installed strong stone vaults which contained the stables. These were likely used to store valuables and food, and as protection against barrages by war engines during sieges. Large cisterns were also built within the keep itself, which provided the residents with a steady and sufficient supply of water during a siege. The two-story keep had an inner courtyard surrounded on all sides by the kitchens, refectory, knights' halls, storerooms, and residential quarters for the soldiers and staff.[56] On the upper floor was a small, limestone chapel and the quarters of the knights themselves, along with the main salon of the fortress commander. Around 50 knights from the Order of the Knights of St. John resided in the castle, along with around 450 militiamen and their families.

The castle resisted one siege by the Muslims in 1180, but two years later, the Battle of Belvoir Castle occurred in the area, between King Baldwin IV of Jerusalem and Saladin. Saladin's response to the caravan raids organized by Reynald of Châtillon was swift and merciless. In 1182 he sent his nephew, Farrukh Shah, northwards from Egypt throughout the Holy Land to bring his armies to Damascus. The Crusaders who were based in the rose-red city of Petra decided to face the Ayyubid army in the deserts of Transjordan, but were unsuccessful in preventing Saladin's forces from reaching Damascus and gaining reinforcements from the emirs of Bosra, Baalbek and Homs.

Eventually, the Crusader armies maneuvered themselves in the vicinity of Belvoir castle, expanding their own forces with soldiers from the many castles in the region. On July 12, 1182, they fought with Saladin's army in the lowlands outside of Belvoir. Using well-practiced tactics, and despite a constant barrage of arrows from Saladin's armies, the infantry and cavalry of the Crusaders overcame the Ayyubid army and forced their leader to flee back to Damascus.

---

[54] Nicolle, 2004
[55] Nicolle, 2004
[56] Nicolle, 2004

Saladin sent more than 12,000 of his soldiers to Galilee via Belvoir following his victory at the Horns of Hattin in 1187. As the other crusader castles and cities in the Holy Land gradually fell to the Arab armies - Sidon, Beirut, Acco, Jaffa, Nazareth and Jerusalem – the few remaining settlements that were held became even more important. By then, all that remained under crusader control was Tyre, Safed, and Belvoir Castle. Saladin's armies besieged Belvoir, and attempted to tunnel their way beneath the outer wall without success – thanks largely to the ingenuity of those who constructed the ramparts.

Because of these setbacks, the siege continued for more than one and a half years, during which time the armies of Saladin experienced substantial losses. Indeed, the siege appeared to never end, and both sides grew weary of the suffering that it entailed. Eventually an agreement was reached between the two forces, in that the Crusader armies would be allowed to safely travel to Tyre in return for relinquishing control of Belvoir to Saladin.

Under Saladin's rule the castle gates and other fortifications were dismantled between 1218 and 1219, fearing that the Crusaders might regain the unconquerable fortress at some point in the future.[57] Indeed, one year after the Arabs finished leveling the fortifications of Belvoir, a Crusader army returned to the area, led this time by King Richard the Lionheart. However, they did not capture the castle on that expedition, and it was not until 1240 that control of the fort was once more held by the Europeans. Due to a lack of funding and manpower the walls and gateway were never restored, and in 1263 the fortress was abandoned. Over time the castle faded into obscurity until excavations in 1966 uncovered the extensive ruins.

Chapter 5: The Decline of Crusader Castles in the 13th Century

"Grace, wisdom and beauty you may enjoy, but beware pride, which alone can tarnish all the rest." - Inscription above the chapel doorway in Krak des Chevaliers[58]

After the crushing defeat against the Crusaders near Belvoir in 1182, Saladin fled to Damascus and subsequently focused his attention on capturing Beirut. The Crusaders organized an enormous fleet at Tyre, with which they managed to force the Ayyubid armies to lift their siege at Beirut. Saladin went on to conquer much of Syria, including the vitally important trade city of Aleppo, before once more directing his forces to the Kingdom of Jerusalem in late 1183. By this point King Baldwin was succumbing to the effects of his leprosy. This led to Guy of Lusignan, husband of Baldwin's sister Sibylla, to be made regent of the kingdom. The Crusaders under Guy of Lusignan suffered a crushing defeat against Saladin's armies at the Horns of Hattin in

---
[57] Nicolle, 2004
[58] "Krak des Chevaliers: Ruined Concentric Crusader Castle in Syria." *Castles and Manor Houses.* (http://www.castlesandmanorhouses.com/page.php?key=Krak%20des%20Chevaliers)

1187, and surrendered Jerusalem to his armies later that year. This loss was a landmark event in the history of the Crusades, leading to an enormous revival in crusading activity in the region and determining the direction of the military campaigns in the 13th and 14th centuries. It also contributed indirectly to the European conquest of other territories, most notably Cyprus and Constantinople.

The loss of Jerusalem – the holiest of cities and crown jewel of the Crusader States – was a catastrophic loss to the Crusaders, and work immediately began to send another crusading army to the Levant to recapture it. Expeditions from England, France, and Germany to the Near East were launched with increasing regularity throughout the 13th century.

The Fourth Crusade from 1202-1204 is significant in medieval history because it was the first time a crusade was directed against another Christian group. It was also significant since it encompassed two of the four major sieges of Constantinople, and it also sparked a third in 1235 (an unsuccessful attempt to reverse the Latin gains in 1204).

Given that legacy, it's ironic that like the Crusades before it, the Fourth Crusade was originally intended as an invasion of Egypt, which had been conquered by Saladin and his uncle nearly four decades earlier. Egypt had been joined with Syria into one Muslim empire under Saladin, but it had fallen apart into two separate realms after his death shortly after the Third Crusade in 1193. Following that crusade, the main objective of the Crusaders in the 13th century was to conquer Egypt and use it as a beachhead against the Muslims in Syria who threatened Christian Palestine, a goal that should have been beneficial to all of Christendom in both the West and East.

Instead, during the Fourth Crusade, tensions between the Latin Christians of Western Europe and the Greek Christians of Constantinople came to a head after a century and three previous Crusades. This resulted in a critical breakdown of communications that resulted in an internal war within Christendom and led to the sack of Constantinople by the Crusaders. After this, the Crusaders established a Latin Kingdom in Constantinople for nearly 60 years, but it remained shaky and was eventually retaken by the Byzantine Greeks.

The Fourth Crusade was also a result of the imperialist ambitions of Pope Innocent III, one of the strongest and proudest popes of the Middle Ages, and it was a precursor of the Albigensian Crusade, the first true "internal" crusade. With that, the Latin Christians began to lose focus on the dwindling territories in Palestine, and instead Christians fell upon each other, engaging in Crusades against other Christian groups and bleeding much-needed support from the Latin kingdoms in Palestine.

In the west, the Fourth Crusade also saw the rise in power of the Byzantines' most bitter rivals in the West: the Venetians and Genoese. The Venetian Doge was later blamed for inciting the Crusaders to fall upon his Byzantine enemies, and while the situation was more complicated than that, the involvement of the Venetians in the altered direction of the Crusade cannot be denied.

Thus, even though no one realized it at the time, the Fourth Crusade was the turning point for the Crusades; after this one, the slow decline toward the Latin Christians losing the Holy Land became inevitable. Constantinople, whether as a Greek or a Latin Empire, was also fatally weakened and would eventually fall to the Ottoman Turks in 1453, long after the end of the Crusades. The Fourth Crusade would inevitably lead to the fall of the Crusader states less than a century later and also the fall of Constantinople two and a half centuries later to the Muslims. The latter would be a permanent loss to Christianity, while Christian forces would not regain control of Palestine until the 20th century.

About a generation later, the Fifth Crusade was defeated at the milestone First Battle of Mansurah in 1221, and although Emperor Frederick II of Germany and Italy became ruler of the Kingdom of Jerusalem in 1225, by the early 1240s the areas around the Holy Land, such as the city of Acre, had become hotbeds of resistance against his rule in Jerusalem.[59] A great transformation occurred in the nature of the Crusading conflict during the later 13th century with the arrival of the Mongol horde from the Central Eurasian steppe in 1243, the rise in power of the Muslim Mamelukes in Egypt, and eventually the rise of the Ottoman Turks in Anatolia. Jerusalem gradually became of lesser importance to the Crusades, which instead focused on staying the spread of Islam into Europe, and in particular via the Balkans.[60]

Known today as Qalaat al-Hosn ("Castle of the Fortress"), Krak des Chevaliers was one of the largest and most important castles occupied during the Crusades in the region of present-day Syria, and it developed a reputation for being impregnable thanks to its colossal defenses. The castle is located a short distance north of *Nahr el-Kebir* ("The Gate of Homs", present-day Emesa), a strategically important mountain pass leading to inland Syria from the Mediterranean coast. It was located there to oversee both the lucrative fishing industry at Lake Homs to the east and the only land-based transport route between Antioch, Beirut and the Mediterranean Sea.

---

[59] Nicolle, 2005
[60] Venning, 2015

Krak des Chevaliers

The first fortress to be established there was erected upon a 650 meter high mountaintop in 1031 by the emir of Homs. This was known as *Hosn al-Akrad* ("Castle of the Kurds"), as it was occupied by a large garrison of Kurdish soldiers during its early years. Over time this name was shortened to "Krak," and after the Crusaders conquered the fortress and began to modify its defenses, its name changed to reflect the new owners, the *chevaliers* ("knights") of the Hospitallers.[61] The castle was captured from the emir of Homs in 1099, during the late expansionist phase of the First Crusade, when Raymond of Toulouse was conquering the region that would later become the County of Tripoli. Raymond instructed his army to strengthen the fortifications of the original castle, which he planned to make use of for his ongoing military ventures in the Levant. They did so, but the castle was subsequently abandoned as the armies of the First Crusade continued south to capture Jerusalem.

The fortress was reclaimed by Tancred, Prince of Galilee, in 1110, and remained a steadfast Crusader stronghold for more than a century. However, by the early 1140s the County of Tripoli was being increasingly threatened by the atabeg of Aleppo and Mosul, a Syrian called Zengi, who had managed to capture the important sites of Hama and Edessa (present-day Sanliurfa) from the Europeans. At that point, the rulers of Tripoli requested that the Order of the Knights of St. John occupy and strengthen *Hosn al-Akrad*. It became the headquarters of the Knights Hospitallers for the rest of the Crusades, and it was at this point that it became known as Krak

---

[61] Nicolle, 2005

des Chevaliers. Further important sites fell to the armies of the Aleppo and Mosul atabeg, including Tortosa and Egypt in 1169. His son, Nur ad-Din, besieged Krak des Chevaliers in 1163, but was unable to conquer it. However, the Knights Hospitallers realized that the castle defenses required improvements, so new high walls and seven impressive round towers, each between eight and ten meters thick, were erected around the central keep – despite a series of earthquakes that delayed the construction work.[62] The main entrance to the fortress was via a long arched gatekeep lined with arrow slits and murder holes above.

Further improvements were made to the castle by the Knights Hospitallers throughout the 13th century, and through their efforts it grew into the largest fortress in the Holy Land. A taller enclosing wall was erected, with a deep and wide moat surrounding it on all sides. At some points the wall exceeded 100 feet in thickness.[63] Massive round towers were constructed at 150 foot intervals along the curtain wall, with narrow slits providing cover for archers in times of siege. Many new structures were established within the main courtyard of the castle, including a bakery, a refectory, a warehouse more than 120 meters long, latrines, and two enormous vaulted stables that could have contained up to a thousand horses.[64] A network of chambers and corridors were also carved into the plateau upon which the castle was built, providing extra storage space for times of siege. The knights constructed two large halls with a beautiful colonnade which were used for meetings and feasts, and a chapel built in a Gothic style reminiscent of their homeland.[65] The Grand Master of the order had his salon in one of the massive towers of the keep. At this point the fortress could contain a population of around two thousand soldiers and staff alongside the fifty or sixty Hospitaller knights stationed there.[66]

Krak des Chevaliers was besieged once again in 1188 by Saladin shortly after he conquered Jerusalem, but yet again the Muslim forces were unable to capture the city. However, in 1269 the Mameluke sultan Baibars, having just conquered Antioch, focused his armies on the County of Tripoli.[67] In March 1271 he approached the Gate of Homs and besieged the colossal castle. Using heavy trebuchets and other siege engines he bombarded the castle walls, and ordered sappers to mine underneath the outer fortifications. The Mameluke troops managed to reach the inner courtyard. Nonetheless, the Knights Hospitallers and their soldiers managed to hold out from within the central keep. Having heard word of the upcoming crusade being led by Prince Edward of England,[68] and being reluctant to completely sack the strategically important fortress

---

[62] Nicolle, 2005
[63] "Krak des Chevaliers: Ruined Concentric Crusader Castle in Syria." *Castles and Manor Houses*. (http://www.castlesandmanorhouses.com/page.php?key=Krak%20des%20Chevaliers)
[64] Folda, J. (1982) "Crusaders Frescoes at Crac des Chevaliers and Marqab Castles." *Dumbarton Oaks Papers*, 36. 177 – 210
[65] Nicolle, 2005
[66] Folda, 1982
[67] Asbridge, 2000
[68] What would later be known as the Ninth Crusade

– no doubt wishing to use it for himself – Sultan Baibars organized a truce with the count of Tripoli. Under their terms, the castle would be surrendered to the Mameluke army, and the Crusader knights within would be granted safe travel to Tripoli.

Under the rule of Baibars some modifications were made to the castle. The walls that had been damaged during the siege were restored, the chapel was converted into a mosque, and two extra towers were erected on the south-western side – a fault in the defenses that he had identified whilst trying to capture the fortress. However, in 1289 the Mameluke forces had managed to conquer Tripoli, Acre and Tortosa in 1291, and the Knights Templar stronghold of Arwad in 1302. These victories meant that the coastal region was relatively securely held, and the strategic importance of Krak des Chevaliers diminished. Eventually the castle was abandoned.

Acre was once one of the most important ports and fortified citadels developed by the Muslims on the Mediterranean Sea. The city had a long and exciting history before the period of the Crusades, being one of the oldest inhabited sites in the Near East. The site was inhabited and developed into a large urban center from at least the 3rd millennium BCE. It was conquered from the Persian Seleucids by Alexander the Great in 332 BCE, and subsequently invaded by King Ptolemy II of Egypt, under whose rule the city was known as Ptolemais.

It was one of the earliest cities to be seized by the Arab Muslims in their conquests of the 7th century.[69] Under their rule it developed into a thriving maritime entrepôt, becoming one of the key trade points and strategic locations in the Umayyad and Abbasid territories.[70] By 861 it had become the main dock at which the Arab warships were constructed and their crews trained. Throughout times of war and relative peace the city was an enormously prosperous site. Located between the Mediterranean, Egyptian, and Middle Eastern spheres, Acre was ideally situated to take advantage of the maritime and land based trade routes crossing Eurasia and North Africa.[71] The revenue acquired by taxing this trade route produced a huge amount of wealth for whoever controlled it. It was for this reason that the city became such an important target before and during the Crusades, being one of the first to be besieged by the European invaders of the First Crusade. After a four year siege the city was conquered by the armies of King Baldwin in 1104.[72] At this point it was renamed St. Jean d'Acre, by which it is known to this day.[73]

---

[69] Jacoby, D. (1982) "Montmussard, Suburb of Crusader Acre: The First Stages of its Development." In *Outremer: Studies in the History of the Crusading Kingdom of Jerusalem presented to Joshua Prawer*. Jerusalem. 205 – 217

[70] Gertwagen, R. (1996) "The Crusader Port of Acre: Layout and Problems of Maintenance." In M. Balard (*ed.*), *Autour de la Première Croisade*. Paris

[71] Gertwagen, 1996

[72] It was only after successfully conquering Acre that King Baldwin's armies continued to Jerusalem, secure in the knowledge that they held the strategically important site.

[73] Sharon, M. (1997) *Corpus Inscriptionum Arabicarum Palaestinae*, Volume A: 1. Leiden: Brill

The Muslim citadel featured a massive labyrinth of alleys and streets that surrounded the fortified castle, accommodating a population of more than quarter of a million by the mid-12th century. [74] The fortifications of the city were built by the Egyptian emir, Ahmad ibn Tulun, whose independent Tulunid dynasty spread into the Abbasid territories of the Levant in the early 870s.[75] In 1187 the city surrendered to Saladin, following the Arab victory at Hattin and capture of Jerusalem.

Acre was ruled by the Ayyubids until 1189, when King Guy of Lusignan, his Frankish armies, and a naval force from Pisa besieged it. Remarkably, the besieging forces at once point found themselves under siege by Saladin's armies – even as they were actively besieging the city on their other flank.[76] After many long years of being besieged, and despite the Arab reinforcements, the city eventually fell to King Guy's troops in July 1191 thanks to the arrival of the armies of King Richard I of England and King Philip II of France. A hospital was founded in Acre during this time, organized by a number of German traders from Lübeck and Bremen. This building became the focal point of the Teutonic Order.[77] The city came under the rule of the Order of the Knights of St. John during the Sixth Crusade.[78] They erected a tremendous Knights Hall, with a vast subterranean crypt, used for ceremonies by the order for more than seven hundred years.

The city was razed by Mameluke invaders in 1291, and the attackers slaughtered every crusader residing in the castle.[79] With its fall came the dissolution of the Latin Kingdom of Jerusalem, a loss that was representative of what had been occurring at castle sites across the Levant as the Christian presence in the Holy Land gradually succumbed to the spread of Muslim armies. The city remained vacant and decrepit until the Ottoman period in the mid-18th century, when a Bedouin sheikh called Zahir al-Umar al-Zaydani made the fortified city the capital of his autonomous territory.[80] He renovated the ruined castle, with further fortifications added by the Ottoman governor Ahmad Pasha al-Jazzar – a man known as "the Butcher" for the effective ambushes he made on the Bedouins.[81] The crusader layer of the city is today obscured by the structures built by the Ottomans, who simply built on top of the pre-existing buildings.

---

[74] Gertwagen, 1996; see also Jacoby, D. (1979) "Crusader Acre in the 13th Century; urban layout and topography." *Studi Medievali*, 20. 1 – 45
[75] Gertwagen, 1996
[76] Sharon, 1997
[77] Sharon, 1997
[78] Peterson, 2001
[79] Gertwagen, 1996
[80] Joudah, A. (2015) "Zahir al-'Umar and the First Autonomous Regime in Ottoman Palestine (1744-1775)" *Jerusalem Quarterly*, 63 – 64.
[81] Philipp, T. (1998) *The Mamluks in Egyptian Politics and Society.* Cambridge University Press

A modern depiction of Zahir al-Umar al-Zaydani by Ziad Daher Zaydany

The Crusading armies gradually shifted their focus away from the Levant during the 13th century, and by the mid-14th century Islamic armies and culture were spreading disturbingly close to the European heartland. Crusading armies were sent to Nicopolis in 1396 to face the Ottomans, but they could not stop Constantinople – the last stronghold of the Christian faith in the Near East – from falling to the Turks in 1453.

As was often the custom in the Middle Ages, the Ottomans were ruthless in their ransacking of the once proud Byzantine capital. The day the Turks got into the city, the streets were full of running blood, women and children were raped or stabbed, and churches, icons, and books were destroyed. The Empire's holiest icon, the virgin Hodegetria, was hacked into four pieces and destroyed. One writer said that blood flowed in the city "like rainwater in the gutters after a sudden storm", and that the bodies of both Turks and Byzantines floated in the sea "like melons along a canal".

The worst massacre was at the Hagia Sophia, where services were underway when the Turks began attempting to raze the church. The Christians shut the great bronze doors, but the Turks smashed their way in. The congregation was all either massacred on the spot or carted away to a

Turkish prison camp. The priests tried to continue with mass until they were killed at the altar. Some Christians believe that a few of them managed to grab the patens and chalices and disappear in to the southern wall of the sanctuary, to wait until the city became a Christian city again, at which time they would resume the service right where it was left off.

Sultan Mehmed had promised his soldiers the traditional three days of looting, but by evening there was nothing left, and he called it off to little protest.

George Sphrantzes, who was in Constantinople when it fell, wrote about the aftermath: "On the third day after the fall of our city, the Sultan celebrated his victory with a great, joyful triumph. He issued a proclamation: the citizens of all ages who had managed to escape detection were to leave their hiding places throughout the city and come out into the open, as they were remain free and no question would be asked. He further declared the restoration of houses and property to those who had abandoned our city before the siege, if they returned home, they would be treated according to their rank and religion, as if nothing had changed."

Perhaps most notably, after the siege was complete, Mehmed, Tursun Bey, the empire's chief ministers, imams, and the Janissaries rode to the Hagia Sophia. Mehmed picked up a handful of earth and sprinkled it over his turban as he entered as a gesture of humility, and as he approached the altar, he stopped one of the soldiers he saw hacking at the building's marble and informed him that looting did not apply to public buildings. He then commanded the senior imam to ascend to the altar and proclaim the name of Allah. With nothing more than the removal of Christian paraphernalia and their replacement with Muslim pulpits and minarets, the legendary Hagia Sophia became a mosque.

The simplicity of the transformation was at once delicate and brutal, as evidenced by the way it's referred to among the Western world and the Turks. In the Christian world, the events are known as "the Fall", but for the Ottomans of history and the Turks of today, it was and remains "the Conquest."

In fairness, the fall of Constantinople was merely the apex of the steady decline. From the mid-13th century fewer new castles were constructed in the Crusader states, and construction had ceased by the 14th century. By the end of the 14th century castles were so strongly defended that successfully capturing one by force was almost out of the question. The only option open then, was a long and drawn out siege where machines of war sat idle until famine and pestilence killed all within the massive stone walls.

As a result of the innovations in medieval warfare, the castle slowly faded from being the focal point of war and lost its well-known role as the defender of the Crusader States. This was due to a wide range of factors. The Crusaders were not able to fully exploit the commercial potential of their estates because of intermittent war and the rise in power of various Mediterranean maritime republics, such as those of Amalfi, Pisa, Genoa, and most importantly Venice. Furthermore, the Mamelukes managed to destroy many of the Crusaders' most important coastal fortifications and ports, and even inland they allowed only a few castles to remain intact. Some castle activity continued on the Kingdom of Cyprus, but because few attackers attempted an invasion of the Mediterranean island even these became redundant due to a lack of technological innovation brought on by conflict.[82]

The emergence of the Ottomans, and of firearm technology, eventually ensured that many castles lost their strategic importance. Nonetheless, the romantic image remains of the Crusaders and Muslim knights as holy warriors in search of glory for God, ruler, and family. Soldiers on both sides resisted hordes of invaders, drove the heathens back from the Holy Land, and did so from some of the most impressive structures ever made by man. Indeed, the influence of Crusader castles extended far beyond the Holy Land. As time went by, fortification design techniques from the east spilled into Europe. Many new features began to be added to the existing castles, and many totally new designs began to appear.

Online Resources

Other medieval history titles by Charles River Editors

Other Crusades titles on Amazon

Bibliography

Munro, DC (1916) The Popes and the Crusades. Proceedings of the American Philosophical Society, 55(5): 348-356

Leclercq, J, F. Vandenbroucke and L. Bouyer (1968) The Spirituality of the Middle Ages. Seabury Press

Constable, G (1996). The Reformation of the 12th Century. Cambridge University Press

Haag, M. (2012) The Tragedy of the Templars: The Rise and Fall of the Crusader States by Michael Haag is published by Profile Books

Jotischky, Andrew (2004) Crusading and the Crusader States. Routledge

Lilie, R (1993) Byzantium and the Crusader States. Oxford University Press

Villehardouin, G (2012). The Conquest of Constantinople. Chronicles of the Crusades.

---

[82] Petre, 2010

Courier Dover Publications

Madden, TF (2005) Crusaders and Historians. First Things

Phillips, J (2005) The Fourth Crusade and the Sack of Constantinople. Penguin

Wintle, Justin (2003) History of Islam. Guidebooks

Queller, DE and Gerald W. Day Some Arguments in Defense of the Venetians on the Fourth Crusade. The American Historical Review, 81 no 4, (1976), 717-737

Queller, DE, Compton, TK and Donald A. Campbell. The Fourth Crusade: The Neglected Majority. Speculum, 49 no 3, (1974), 441-465

Tyerman, C (2004) God's War: A New History of the Crusades. Penguin

Harris, Jonathan (2014) Byzantium and the Crusades. Bloomsbury

Bird, J, E. Peters and JM Powell (2013) Crusade and Christendom: Annotated Documents in Translation from Innocent III to the Fall of Acre, 1187-1291. University of Pennsylvania Press

Brand, CM (1962) The Byzantines and Saladin, 1185-1192: Opponents of the Third Crusade. Speculum, 37(2): 167-181

Jacoby, D. (1973) The Encounter of Two Societies: Western Conquerors and Byzantines in the Peloponnesus after the Fourth Crusade. The American Historical Review, 78(4): 873-896

Housley, N (1984) King Louis the Great of Hungary and the Crusades, 1342-1382. The Slavonic and East European Review, 62(2): 192-208

Cahen, C (1954) An Introduction to the First Crusade. Past & Present, 6: 6-30

Fotheringham, JK (1910) Genoa and the Fourth Crusade. The English Historical Review, 25(97): 26-57

Munro, DC (1931) The Western Attitude toward Islam during the Period of the Crusades. Speculum, 6(3): 329-343

Runciman, S (1951) History of the Crusades: Volume I, The First Crusade and the Foundation of the Kingdom of Jerusalem. Cambridge University Press

Runciman, S (1951a) History of the Crusades: Volume II, The Kingdom of Jerusalem. Cambridge University Press

Housley, Norman (2003) The Italian Crusades. Ashgate

Lock, Peter. (2013) The Routledge Companion to the Crusades. Routledge

Kedar, B.Z., ed. *The Horns of Hattin*. London: Variorum, 1992.

Tyerman, Christopher, ed. *Chronicles of the First Crusade*. New York: Penguin Books, Ltd., 2011.

Tyerman, Christopher. *The Debate on the Crusades, 1099-2010*. Manchester [UK]: Manchester University Press, 2011.

Rees, Tom J. *The First Crusade: An Overview*. 1999. http://www.brighton73.freeserve.co.uk/firstcrusade/Overview/Overview.htm

Asbridge, Thomas. *The First Crusade: A New History*. Oxford [UK]: Oxford University Press, 2004. http://books.google.com/books/about/The_First_Crusade.html?id=sIJlMsv8gVIC

Chamberlin, John V. *Imagining Defeat: An Arabic Historiography of the Crusades*. Thesis for Excelsior College, 2007. http://www.dtic.mil/cgi-bin/GetTRDoc?AD=ADA467268

Gabrieli, Francesco. *Arab Historians of the Crusades*. London: Routledge and Keegan Paul Ltd., 1969 (Originally published in Italian in 1957). http://books.google.com/books/about/Arab_Historians_of_the_Crusades.html?id=JU0eSxDCOmIC

Hillenbrand, Carole. *The Crusades: Islamic Perspectives*. Edinburgh [UK]: Edinburgh University Press, 1999. books.google.com/books?isbn=0415929148

Laiou, Angeliki E. and Mottahedeh Roy P. *The Crusades from the Perspective of Byzantium and the Muslim World*. Washington, D.C.: Dunbarton Oaks, 2001. http://books.google.com/books?id=YTAhPw3SjxIC

Maalouf, Amin. *The Crusades Through Arab Eyes*. New York: Al Saqi Books, 1984. https://www.google.com/search?tbm=bks&hl=en&q=The+crusades+through+arab+eyes&btnG=

Madden, Thomas. *The New Concise History of the Crusades*. Lanham [MD]: Rowman and Littlefield Publishers, Inc., 2005. http://books.google.com/books/about/The_New_Concise_History_Of_The_Crusades.html?id=fKYxKsgVpmMC

Riley-Smith, Jonathan. *The First Crusade and Idea of Crusading*. London: The Athlone Press, 1995 (originally published in 1986). http://books.google.com/books/about/The_First_Crusade_and_Idea_of_Crusading.html?id=RNP6MBmn-2EC

Runciman, Steven. *The First Crusade*. Cambridge [UK]: Cambridge University Press, 1980. http://books.google.com/books/about/The_First_Crusade.html?id=Z_sWBOzEleMC

Free Books by Charles River Editors

We have brand new titles available for free most days of the week. To see which of our titles are currently free, click on this link.

Discounted Books by Charles River Editors

We have titles at a discount price of just 99 cents everyday. To see which of our titles are currently 99 cents, click on this link.